HENRY NELSON WRIGHT

1869 - 1941

NUMISMATIST

INDIAN CIVIL SERVANT

An account of his Life

by

his great grand daughter

JUDY URQUHART

ISBN: 9798842868667

INTRODUCTION

Henry Nelson Wright, was an expert on Mughal coins whose collection is now in the British Museum in London. He also wrote books on the subject and was a founder of the Indian Numismatic Society. Coins gradually took over from his original career, as an Officer in the Judiciary of the Indian Civil Service, and became his passion.

Henry was born on 29 October 1869, the son of Francis Nelson Wright a District Commissioner with the ICS. The place of his birth was thought to be Priory Road, Kew though recent Ancestry searches say it was in Manipur in the North Eastern Province in India.

BACKGROUND

The Wright family seem to have originated in Warwickshire. In the family Bible the first Wright to be mentioned is William Wright DCL of Edgbaston in Warwickshire. He married on June 25, 1834 Mary Goddard Townsend at All Saints Church in Cambridge.

There is more information relating to Mary Goddard Townsend and her background listed on separate sheets in the Bible owned by Ian Nelson Wright. The records start in 1697. The place is Stanstead. The name John Townsend. His daughter Sarah married a Richard Streatfield at Otford in Kent in the early 1750's. They had four children, Sarah, Richard, Nicholas and William. And so the line divides and descends until a traceable line begins in the early 19th century for my great grandfather's branch of the family with the marriage of the said Mary Goddard Townsend to William Wright.

William Wright was educated in Cambridge. He joined the church and the Rev. Wright is first listed as Schoolmaster of Huddersfield but then became a professor at University College School in London and subsequently headmaster of the Royal Grammar School, Colchester in Essex. The couple had eleven children – five boys and six girls. Three died in infancy. The third child was christened Francis Nelson and he was born in 1840 on November 17 in Belgrave Terrace, Huddersfield.

Francis was clever. He won a King's Scholarship to Eton. The Eton School Register 1853-1859 Part 11 lists: WRIGHT K.S. Francis Nelson ICS son of W.W., Schoolmaster of Huddersfield 1852-1859,: Coll Wall 1858; Exeter Coll. Oxford, B.A. formerly Magistrate and Collector N.W. Provinces of Indian. Opium Agent, Benares.

King's Scholars at Eton used to take an entrance exam between the ages of 10 and 14. They had to satisfy the authorities of their proficiency in Latin translation, Latin Grammar, French Grammar, Arithmetic, outlines of English, History and Geography. To these the headmaster had the power to add Latin composition in Prose and Verse, Greek Grammar and translation, Elementary Algebra, the higher rules of Arithmetic and elements of Geometry. Every boy admitted was placed in school according to the result of the above examination. Once there the Sciences, natural sciences, sports, music, drama and philosophy could be added to the curriculum.

King's Scholars lodged in the Long Chamber and New Buildings adjoining the College. The first fifty five got separate rooms the remainder sleeping apartments in Long Chamber. Scholars were boarded at the expense of the College. Provost and Fellows might from time to time fix an annuity to this sum but not to exceed £30. No Scholar could be absent from College for more than six months without special permission of Provost and Fellows. The Provost in Francis Wright's time was Rev. Francis Hodgson and then Rev. Edward Craven Hawtrey.

After leaving Eton, Francis took the Indian Civil Service exam; perhaps taking advantage of the opening up of the entry exam to boys other than those who had completed their education with two years at Hailebury. His career was spent in the Indian Civil Service and he rose to become District Commissioner for the United Provinces. A large, handsome man – judging from photographs – he married a woman called Florence on 11 September, 1863 at St. John, Fitzroy. They produced seven children – 5 boys and 2 girls. The first two, both sons Francis and Charles, died in infancy.

BEGINNINGS

The third son, christened Henry Nelson was born on 29 October in 1869. Priory Road, Kew was generally thought to be the place of his birth and that perhaps his parents were home on leave. However recent Ancestry searches say he was born in Manipur in the North East Province of India.

After Henry came two girls with whom he remained close. Amelia Florence Catherine known as Florrie was born on April 22, 1872 and Ethel Mary Frances known as Polly was born around 6 July, 1874. Then came a boy Edward Cyril 7 July 1876 and another boy William who died in infancy.

Henry took after his father and had brains. He too won a King's scholarship to Eton in 1883. The Eton School Register, Part V. 1883-1889 lists him as: WRIGHT K.S., EDS & JC Henry Nelson son of Francis Nelson Wright of the Bengal Civil Service, 1883-1888, Coll Wall 1886-7 Mixed Wall 1887. Exhibnr of Corpus Christie College Oxford, Indian Civil Service, Registrar of the High Court Allahabad, India. Mar. Edith Mary d. of George Stuckey. Firwood, Clevedon Somerset.

All scholars were supposed to be as good at games as they were in the class room and in Henry's case this was true. He played the Eton Wall Game becoming a member of both the College Wall and Mixed Wall Game Teams. The Captains of the teams wrote Reports of the games on blue paper in a book contained in the Eton archive. Henry played in the Outsider position and, in the St. Andrew's Day match of 1885 of Collegers against Oppidons, G. Marshall, The Keeper described the day: 'This match was played as usual on St. Andrew's Day. The weather was all that could be desired and the wall in striking contrast to last year, was in first rate condition: the attendance, therefore, of spectators was unprecedentedly large and they were rewarded by seeing a splendid contest and match... The 2nds played well and Fernard and Wright were good. The game throughout was played in the most friendly spirit.'

Then on Oct 11 in the Mixed Wall match of The School v. Veterans, 'Thorold, Thellusson and Wright did most where all did well' and on Saturday September 24 1887 in 'A capital game for the 1st Saturday in the Half ....Wright played excellently.' While on November 17th there was 'some dashing play by the Outsiders' whose numbers included 'For the Collegers' among others 'Wright'.

In 1888 Henry finished school and went up to Oxford on a Brasenose Exhibition to Corpus Christie College. Before starting at Oxford he took the Indian Civil Service entrance exam in 1888 and passed out near the top. It was common practice to sit the exam before doing a two year probationary stint at University. Balliol College, Oxford being the most popular. Henry's grandson Tony Condon says 'He was a very brainy chap. Took the Civil Service Exams. At that time the ICS was more prestigious than the Home Civil Service.' Of Henry's year at Eton only one other is listed as going into the ICS. Several were destined for the Indian Army but most were bound for the South African War except for those with Country Estates. At Oxford Henry continued to play games and was photographed as a member of the cricket team. He is reported to have been an excellent tennis player and an early entrant at Wimbledon.

Henry would have studied Classics. The subject was considered the best preparation for public life. Latin's 'hard logicality and economy of words taught good judgement and precise language'. Learning about the Classical Greek masters such as Plato and Aristotle 'provided justification for rule by an elite' but he would also have been taught political economy, history and Indian languages.

Exams punctuated his early career in the Indian Civil Servant. As he progressed there were more exams in law and the vernaculars. Tests kept the standards high for 'the Heaven born', as those in The Indian Civil Service were termed, for their belief that 'a greater and more admirable work' had never been 'conceived in any country' and that it was 'for the lasting benefit of the human race'. The British might make mistakes and were sometimes hard, insolent and overbearing but no government in the world rested on 'so secure a moral basis' or was 'more fiercely animated by duty.'

INDIA

His good marks in the ICS exam combined with, no doubt, his fathers influence guaranteed that Henry was immediately posted to the best positions in the Indian Civil Service. He was also following in a tradition of families who served India for generations with siblings often working in several of the different services. A brother might be in the ICS, another in the Army or Indian Medical Service and sisters married to fellow members.

On 2 September 1890 Henry formally joined the Service and sailed for India. Before leaving England he had to equip himself with a long, expensive list of the correct clothes for work, a social life and a sporting one. His voyage crossed the Mediterranean and passed through the Suez Canal and arrived in Bombay three weeks later on 29 October. A period known as 'joining time' was allowed for the new recruit to travel to his appointed destination. In the Civil Service List Henry is described as: 'attached and served in the N.W. Provinces and Oudh as assistant magistrate and collr. (now UIttar Pradesh) Wright, Henry Nelson, Judge, U.P. of Agra and Oudh.'

British India came to consist of nine provinces and various parcels of territory including Rajputana and Baluchistan – the latter nominally ruled by a Maharaja but with British involvement in the form of a resident Political Officer. All the main administrative and judicial posts were occupied by members of the Indian Civil Service, but they were all ruled differently, the British matching their laws to the customs of the country. These provinces were divided into smaller sections presided over by a Commissioner of the Division and under him Magistrates and Collectors and their Deputies all of whom were responsible for smaller sections of territory. So, as you rose up the ranks of the ICS, you came to command ever larger pieces of land and people. The officers were responsible for collecting rents, settling disputes over land and behaviour and generally ensuring the country and its inhabitants remained peaceful, law abiding, productive and produced taxes for the State. There were High Courts in Calcutta, Madras, Bombay and Allahabad for settling disputes. The North Western Provinces and the Punjab were the most favoured destinations and got the best recruits, while the least popular, Madras and Bombay, got the worst or 'bad bargains'.

The N.W. Province had advantages; the climate was drier and healthier; there were more people and therefore a more extensive and varied social life - much of it provided by British officers and their families quartered in garrisons such as Meerut and Cawnpore. Civilians liked the local inhabitants, their language and masculinity, and they admired the towns, the Mughal monuments at Agra, the decadent beauty of Lucknow, the Hindu pilgrimage centre at Allahabad. There was an abundance of sport, shooting and pig sticking were plentiful.

Henry's first posting was Meerut. He started on 6 November 1890 as Assistant Magistrate and Collector. Meerut was an important garrison town, about sixty kilometres north of Delhi, spread along the shores of the river Ganges, bordered by temples, dharmsalas and sati pillars. The town was where the 'fire' that sparked the Mutiny of 1857 was lit, 'the conflagration that spread like wild fire across the parched gangetic plain and deep into the forest scrub of Central India'.

Raw recruits were known as Griffins and expected to learn on the job from the Collector to whom he was attached.

The Collectors taught by example the principles of administration and gave practical advice about co-operation between the different services and departments. Very often the recruit lodged with the Collector and his wife until they found their feet though, in the larger stations where there were several bachelors, they might club together in 'chummeries' to save costs and loneliness. In a station everyone knew each other and were interested in the doings or failings of their neighbours. Friendships made were frequently dislocated by transfers to other districts.

A griffin's first months were divided between studying for his departmental exams and doing whatever minor jobs his District Office assigned him. In the cold weather the DO might take him on a tour of the district, showing him villages and introducing him to the mysteries of land settlement and revenue assessment. In summer he might be in the treasury to learn the system of revenue accounts. Until he passed his departmental exams, the griffin possessed third grade magisterial powers that allowed him to impose small fines and prison sentences. Language, judiciary, revenue and treasury were the staples of departmental exams.

A year later, on 15 December 1891, Henry officially went on Survey Duty in Roorkee. This town, standing on a ridge overlooking the Solani River, had grown from a mud village in 1845 to be a manufacturing town and military station and headquarters of the Ganges Canal workshop and iron foundry with its own civil engineering college.

Page   13

MARRIAGE

Early in 1892, Henry traveled down to Madras to marry Edith Stuckey. She was related to the West Country Banking dynasty. Stuckey's Bank originated in Langport in Somerset in the 18th century and grew to rival the Bank of England. It was said that 'the Somerset farmer is never satisfied as long as he has a Bank of England Note in his pocket...until he has changed it for one of Stuckey & Co., which he holds with confidence until the day of his death.' The most illustrious family member was Walter Bagehot, the political economist who was first editor of the Economist magazine and wrote books on finance and the constitution still quoted today. Bagehot's mother was called Edith Stuckey.

The exact origins of Henry's fiancé Edith Stuckey are shrouded in mystery. There is a story that she was Italian and indeed her dark good looks do speak of Latin roots. However she is described as being the only daughter of George Stuckey and was brought up by her spinster aunt Mary Ann Phillips Stuckey. George is another recurring Stuckey name but this one was last heard of in Melbourne, Australia.

My theory is that George married an Italian who died in child birth. The baby daughter was taken in by her aunt, George's sister, while he went off to seek his fortune in Australia – perhaps in the gold fields round Melbourne or to establish a branch of the bank. The area was notoriously lawless at the time and, whatever happened, George was never heard of again.

Edith lived with her aunt in the respectable Sneyd Park area of Bristol but where she was educated and where she met Henry is unknown. Were they were already engaged before she set sail for India?. There is no record of any Stuckey's in Madras at the time, though a manager of the Bank in Bath had been a member of the Council in Madras and so perhaps there were connections.

If Henry already knew Edith before leaving England, and they were engaged, perhaps they waited for him to establish himself in India before getting married. Henry was only twenty three and Edith presumably much the same age. This was young to get married in the days when it was frowned upon by the ICS to marry before your late twenties. Early marriage, it was considered, could hamper a career. The prevailing opinion was that it made a man poorer and less mobile and could ruin his prospects. 'Don't marry until you have had five years service' was the general advice generally given. But Henry ignored the advice.

There is an announcement from the 1982 Madras newspaper: '24 February – married Edith Stuckey only daughter of George Stuckey Esq. of Sneyd Park, Clifton, Bristol to Henry Nelson Wright, Bengal Civil Service, son of F.N. Wright Esq. C.S. Commissioner Allahabad. At St. George's Cathedral, Madras. By the Revd. Archdeacon Elwes, assisted by the Revd. W. Parker.'

Madras was the first settlement made in India by the East India Company in the 17th century, a handsome town of colonial buildings strung along the water front and harbour. St. George's Cathedral was built later, in the early 19th century, and situated on the north side of the town. It is described in the Murray Guide 1933 as standing in 'an enclosure on the E. side of the gardens. The exterior is not handsome, but the dazzling white chunam, the decorated roof, the very numerous and remarkably handsome tablets and tombs, and the lofty and massive pillars in the interior, produce a very pleasing impression.'

The couple returned to Meerut and presumably set up house and began what appears a happy marriage that lasted 24 years and produced four children Isola, Harcourt, Innes and Trevor.

They are thought to have gone on honeymoon in Italy a year later in 1893. Perhaps if the theory that Edith's mother was Italian is correct then it could have been to visit her birthplace or even relations. They had, if I am imagining correctly, an idyllic time staying on Lake Garda – the largest of the Italian lakes – and sailed out on the steamer to the island in the middle – Isola Bella. Was it during this visit to Lake Garda that their first child was conceived. A girl they christened Isola, after the island, was born in 1894 at Meerat.

Their life of an Indian Civil Servant and his wife continued at Meerat. Edith's pride in the progress of her family can be seen in a series of grand photographs that she must have commissioned. Judging by the ones in Ian Nelson Wright's collection, which are undated, it looks as though it became almost an annual event for the family to dress up in their best clothes and pose for a group portrait. They are formal, yet relaxed and show an affectionate and growing family. To begin with it is just Henry and Edith. He is a neat looking man with keen eyes and fairish coloured hair and small moustache, sitting beside his dark, rather beautiful and fashionably dressed wife. Then they are joined by baby Isola in 1892 and later by the other children, Harcourt 1899, Innes 1902 and Trevor 1906. They look confident and at ease with each other and their lives. There is a settled contentment about the family. Edith and Henry appear well suited.

The pictures show their circumstances. They wear formal clothes, in Edith's case it was an elaborate dress, and sit in armchairs in the garden and surrounded by a retinue of servants.

They have tea on the lawn before a large white stucco bungalow and tall Indian trees. They are on horses before the house as if setting out for a morning ride. They are present at a meet for the hunt of perhaps wild boar or a drag hunt, among a large crowd, immaculately dressed on equally well groomed horses. They go to garden parties, the women in beautiful long Edwardian dresses, waited on by swooping Indian servants in turbans. They play tennis and badminton. Henry competes in team games, he is seated with his fellow players. Henry was especially good at tennis winning a Blue at Oxford and being an early competitor at Wimbledon He joins the volunteer force.

In many of the photographs taken during the 1890's there is Henry's sister, Florence looking decorative and pretty and a rotund, prosperous looking man. He is Harcourt Butler; a rising star at the Allahabad Law Courts.

Harcourt Butler was born in 1869, the second of nine sons of Spencer Percival Butler a barrister of Lincoln's Inn. He was educated at Harrow and then Balliol College Oxford. Several of his brothers also went on to have notable careers, and his nephew Rab almost became Conservative prime minister in the 1960's.

Harcourt was to have a highly distinguished career, twice Governor of Burma and Lieutenant Governor of the United Provinces and author of influential reforms to the government of India for famine relief, education and agrarian unrest. He was also a highly cultivated man, a master of the pithy phrase delivered with wit and style. 'He had a brilliant intellect, boundless energy and wonderful capacity for getting at the root of the matter, ability to express his conclusions....and a very practical head in carrying them out. Butler was a wonderful host. His fondness for music added greatly to the charm of his entertainments'. He made Lucknow, the capital of Oudh, his own and 'enhanced the beauties and amenities of the capital.' Indeed a Palace was built for him by the Raja Ali Khan of Mahmudabad Palace, Butler Palace still exists in Lucknow although in a very dilapidated state.

He became friends with the Nehru family and it was in their home city of Allahabad that he began his service with the ICS. Harcourt arrived in India at the same time as Henry and it seems likely they met at Oxford. The friendship remained important and lasted for their lives.

Henry moved to Dehra Dun on 2nd November 1893 where he is registered as Assistant Magistrate and Collector and that he was on Examination Leave between 31 March and 4 April 1894. The town of Dehra Dun is 'prettily situated in the midst of a mountain valley 2300 ft above sea level under the foothills of the Himalayas. Home of the Indian Forest College, the Indian Military Academy and the Doon School. It was taken by the British in 1815 and since then enjoyed a great reputation as a hill resort'

Florence married Harcourt Butler in Dehra Dun in July 1894. Did this mean that she was living with her brother before she married? Their mother had died. When is not known but their father had married again, Amelia Hannah Barnes who died in 1884 or 8 when he took another wife, a widow. On 4th July 1893 it was announced, the marriage took place of 'Francis Nelson Wright, BCS commissioner, Allahabad to Emily Latham Curling, youngest daughter of late Sir Douglas Forsyth, KCSI, CB, BCS, All Saints Cathedral, Allahabad by Rev. G.H. Ingle.

Did this fact influence Florence in her decision to accept Harcourt's proposal? And did the fact that her beloved brother had married two years earlier, although there is no evidence that she was not good friends with his wife Edith. More telling perhaps was that, with her father's remarriage, a step mother would have taken over the home.   Perhaps Florence felt usurped. Perhaps she wanted to leave home and establish one of her own.   Women were nothing without a husband in those days.   Perhaps she was flattered by the proposal from the rising star and assumed because he was a friend of her brother's he would somehow be the same.

But it is debatable that she was in love with Harcourt. The marriage foundered from the start. In any description of Harcourt's life she makes only brief appearances.   It seems they lived apart almost from day one of their married life. In The Ruling Caste David Gilmour asserts that 'Harcourt Butler had a wife who even abandoned him temporarily of their wedding day. Butler's marriage did not improve after her return' and when Harcourt became Lieutenant Governor of the United Provinces 'he confided to his Under-Secretary that, although he had been married to his wife for many years, they had not lived together for more than eight days. Lady Butler gave an order to the same official: "Mr. Lupton, never leave me in the room with Harcourt". Perhaps Florence found no physical desire for the fat man and became repulsed by his licentious behaviour and court of women which, to give him credit, he could have been driven by her rejection.

However there was a son Victor, born in 1900 so there must have been some form of union. Both mother and son outlived Harcourt. Florence returned to London and lived in a series of flats in Chelsea and Earls Court looked after by a maid and a cook and financially supported by Harcourt.

Victor followed the family tradition and was educated at Harrow and Magdalene College Oxford. He became a stock broker and then entered the Civil Service in 1940 as Under Secretary at the Ministry of Fuel and Power, ending his career as senior executive with Shell Oil and dying on 19th June 1969 while on holiday at the Queen's Hotel in Penzance.

Meanwhile, the other sister Polly never married. It was said she was thwarted in love by her father and left England, vowing never to return, and made her life first in Berlin and then in Montreux in Switzerland. The youngest, Cyril E. Nelson Wright was a rising star in the Navy who married a Miss Swabey, the daughter of the Archbishop of the Lee and Windward Islands and was killed while playing Polo in Gibraltar in 1914.

ASIATIC SOCIETY

Henry was elected to the membership of the Asiatic Society on 30th August, 1894. The Asiatic Society was formed in Calcutta by the great scholar and Orientalist, Sir William Jones at the end of the 18th century and had a practical monopoly on new learning. The Headquarters were established in Calcutta and Scholars of the day were active members of the Society and pioneered the Sanskrit Renaissance just as the Greek Scholars of the 15th C. had revived learning in Europe. The Asiatic Society defined their range of inquiries to extend to 'whatever is performed by man or produced by nature'. The Asiatic Society was the solid organ of research in Asia. It instigated investigations into Geology, Meteorology, Zoology and Botany. The results of their research were all published in the Journal. As time went on all these branches grew and developed and specialized along lines of their own. They 'multiplied by fission' and gave birth to the Geological Survey, Meteorological Survey, Botanic Survey, Indian Museum Linguistic Survey and Numismatics. Thus 'the Parent is rather depleted'.

Civilians who liked books and talking about books, who wanted to keep their brains active, found little opportunity. They worked long hours and as their duties piled up they had less time and inclination for serious reading and usually relaxed with games or sport. As 'he found himself sinking into dullness and absorption in his work' some studied Indian history, religion, ethnology and anthropology in order to prevent themselves 'growing into an Anglo-Indian bore with no knowledge of anything outside his shop.' It was said that the only cure for a civilian who could not think of anything but work was to take up an abstruse subject – one that took some tackling but 'could never be any possible use to you in your profession.' But it could also come from a genuine interest in India and its culture and a realization that you were there for life.

COINS

Henry chose coins. He joined the Asiatic Society. In 1902 the Council of the Asiatic Society authorized the addition of a Numismatic Supplement to the three parts of the Journal. It was decided to 'publish short notes on numismatic questions with illustrations, as a Supplement to the Journal, Part 5 and the Editorship has been entrusted to Mr. H. Nelson Wright I.C.S.'

A Coins Committee was established. Henry was one of ten members - listed in alphabetical order starting with Lt. Col. D.S.E. Bain and ending with The Hon. Mr. John Hooper and including the redoubtable Babu Panchanan Mukerjee in its ranks Joining the Society marked a turning point in Henry's life. From then on his interest in coins grew until it became the main focus of his life.

In a letter to myself dated 8 June, 1995 from Dr. Parmeshuari Lal Gupta of the Indian Institute of Research in Numismatic Studies (P.O. Anjanery, Dist. Nasik, Maharashtra) - whose name was given to me by the British Museum with the advice to write soon as he was now very old but he was a great scholar and could well remember Nelson Wright - said 'How and when Mr. Wright acquired interest in Indian numismatics, I do not know, however I presume he might have acquired interest in it when he was one of the Secretaries of the Asiatic Society of Bengal (I Park Street, Calcutta). In those days, the Society was entrusted to look after the coins that were being found in North India and dealt with under the Treasure Trove Act. Mr. Wright would have had to see those coins as the Secretary of the Society.'

It was Mr. C.J. Rogers of Amritsar who, between 1880 and 1895, was the first to attempt to describe coin types and inscriptions. Mint lists show historians what places were included in the Mughal Empire at various periods, and act as a guide to the numismatist in ascertaining whether a coin of a particular mint is known or not known. However, systematic and scientific work in the field of Mughal numismatics date from the appearance of the tables compiled by R. Burn ICS . 'Under the impetus of his excellent example research has proceeded at a rapid rate'. The first Numismatic Supplement appeared in 1904 under the editorship of Henry Nelson Wright

PROMOTION IN THE ICS

Meanwhile Henry's career progressed up the Indian Civil Service ladder. His move to Allahabad is recorded on 9 March 1895 where he is still listed as Assistant Magistrate and Collector.

Allahabad was the official capital of the United Provinces until this was moved to Agra. It was in Allahabad that Lord Canning held his famous Durbar, after the suppression of the Mutiny, when Queen Victoria's proclamation announcing the transfer of the government of India from the East India Company to the Crown was read. It then became the seat of the Provincial Administration. In 1902 the N.W. Provinces and Oudh were amalgamated as the United Provinces of Agra and Oudh under a Lieutenant-Governor who was replaced in 1920 by a Governor. There is a University and a High Court where early on Indians sat with British judges. Motilal Nerhu, father of Pandit, first President of India was a Judge. The family lived in Allahabad and it was from here they fought for Independence.

Allahabad is situated on a wedge of land at the meeting point of the rivers Jumna and Ganges and as such is regarded as a holy place. The city was built by Akbar in 1583 on the site of an ancient Hindu city. The place is believed to be sacred and pilgrims flock to bathe in the Ganges every year at the Magh Mela and every twelve years at the Kumbh Mela   It received the name Allahabad in 1584 and made capital of the Province. The Emperor Jehangir lived and governed from the Fort as did his son and successors.

Was it in Allahabad that Henry began his specialized study of the Mughals and their coins? Whatever, he was still travelling. On 4 September he was in Banda. This town stood on an undulating plain on the bank of the river Ken. 'The three characteristics of Banda are its liability to agricultural calamity, its trade in the cutting and polishing of precious stones, and its facilities for shooting panther, bear and sambhar.' Then it was back to Allahabad on 18 October and then, on 5 November, he was appointed Joint Magistrate. The following year on 6 April he was in Shahjahanpur which was the chief town of a district with a civil station, cantonment station and several churches.

There was also an Army Clothing Factory, the Rosa Sugar Factory, a rum distillery and 'The city also produced excellent silk cloth'. Besides which 'Good duck shooting is in the Shajahanpur district; the forests in the N. are full of spotted deer.

Then, On 23 April 1896, he received the significant promotion to Under Secretary to the Government   Some ninety Civilians about a tenth of the ICS worked at desks in Calcutta, Simla or the provincial capitals.   Most were secretaries of some kind; Under Secretaries and Chief Secretaries of local governments, the departments of the Government of India and sometimes Private Secretaries to the Viceroy.   In the NWP the Chief Secretary would aspire to membership of the Board of Revenue and even to the Lieutenant Governorship.

Few refused a Secretariat because it was difficult to get to the top without some experience of the bureaucracy. Under Secretaries had to acquire a full dress uniform in dark blue embroidered with gold and a sword and cocked hat.

Their work instead of dealing with people and crops changed to reading reports and writing minutes often for ten hours a day. Many found the change in circumstances a relief and 'used to feel a throb of pure pleasure on coming into a large cool quiet office room with mountains of papers scientifically filed by a first-rate Head Clerk on each side of an armchair.' These files proceeded in leisurely way round the district Secretariats: 'like the diurnal revolution of the earth went the file, stately, solemn, sure and slow; and now, in due season, it has completed its orbit, and I (Curzon) am invited to register the concluding stage.'

The secretariat were often resented by the District Officers who felt they received inadequate reward for toiling all year in the plans while they lived congenially among their fellow countrymen. They were irritated by the 'Secretaries' self confidence, their assumption that they were always justified in imposing their views on men on the spot. They might have had the "paper knowledge" on a subject but not the practical experience. Secretaries seldom worked outside their district because without knowing the population in his charge, the individuals, the castes, the religions, he could not perform his work.

Henry worked until January 1899. From 2 February to 1 November he took nine months Subsidiary leave. This was normally granted for 'urgent private affairs' - the death of a parent or ordering affairs after the death of a wife. For what reason did Henry take it and where did they stay? Perhaps with Edith's aunt in Bristol. She did not officially take the lease of Firwood in Clevedon until 1906 - after which the house became the family's base in Britain - and so perhaps if she was still living in Sneyd Park in Bristol that is where they stayed. Did they leave Isola behind with her when they returned in November to be educated in England?

Edith was pregnant. Perhaps they came home for her to give birth. A son was born on 3rd May 1899 at Priory Road, Kew and christened Aislerby Harcourt. The second name given for their great friend Harcourt Butler who was also Godfather to the boy. Cracks in Harcourt's marriage to Florence do not appear to have affected his friendship with Henry.

On his return to India Henry was promoted to Director of Land Records & Agriculture and Joint Secretary to the Board of Revenue on 5 November. This was an important departmental post. Then on 21 February 1901 he was appointed Registrar of the High Court in Allahabad.

His grandson Tony Condon said that 'eventually in the ICS there came a time when you specialized and went either into the Administrative side of the Service or into the Judiciary. Henry choose the latter route, ending up at the High Court in Allahabad.'

The law courts in India had a massive amount of work. Nearly 2 million people were arraigned each year in the criminal courts, nearly 3 million suits were bought before the civil courts. A complex network of judges with different duties and functions was required to deal with these case. A good number of cases came before the Magistrates of the ICS but since they possessed only limited powers of sentencing the more serious went up to the Sessions Court. Murders were tried by a Session Judge whereas the important civil suits were tried by a District Judge. Above them were the High Courts of Calcutta, Bombay, Madras and Allahabad. They were well paid – 48.000 rupees.

A High Court Judge, once he had managed to get on top of his work, usually enjoyed a life of more leisure and less stress than that of a District Officer. He did not tour or go on circuit. His days work ended with the closing of the court room door. Fixed hours meant he had free time for his other interests. Many took the path to the Judiciary with this in mind.

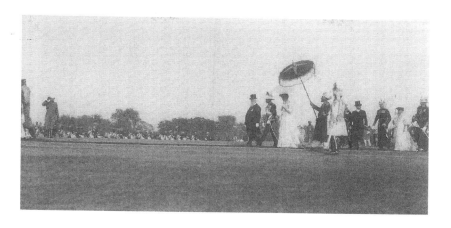

Durbar for King Edward VII in 1906

Henry and Edith moved in the top echelons of society. There are photographs of them at Durbars – the one for Edward Vll in 1906.- and they continued to appear beautifully dressed at garden parties and tennis parties and playing badminton. Polo was a popular sport and hunting – shooting for the pot the abundant game in India. A man could 'stalk his way through the season of duck, deer, jungle fowl, peacock, snipe, partridge and quail. There was large game in the form of wild boar. It was regarded as second only to fox hunting but more dangerous.' There were also drag hunts. Henry was a member of sporting teams, played cricket and polo and joined the volunteer army.

Page   34

NUMISMATICS

His fascination with coins and their interpretation was gaining ground. The Asiatic Society journal published intermittent supplements devoted to the specialized study of a subject. As has been stated, in 1902 Henry was appointed editor of the Asiatic Journal Supplement on coins. The 1st Supplement appeared in 1904. 'Mr. Wright as the Secretary of the Asiatic Society of Bengal had decided in 1904 to issue a supplement of the Journal of the Society, which is known as 'Numismatic Supplement', to publish papers exclusively related to numismatics and thus to organize the Numismatic Studies. He took upon himself to edit the Supplements. Soon he realized that coin-collecting was being perused haphazardly by individuals, mostly by government officers and only a few others. There was no co-ordination between them. 'He took interest towards organizing them and a conference was organized at Allahabad (U.P.) 28 December 1910 at the residence of the District Magistrate.'

Coins are important clues to the history and organization of early societies. Through coins you can tell the rise of cities and civilizations, the movement of people and armies, their rulers and their courts and what they hold valuable. But to decipher early coins takes immense scholarship and background knowledge of the language, culture and habits of the people you are studying. Even the lunar calendar must be studied and a knowledge of Persian and Arabic and its calligraphy is essential

Henry focused on the coins of the Mughal Empire in India. As he says in the Preface to The Sultans of Dehli and Mediaeval Muhammadem States, 1907: 'A reliable index to the geographical limits of the empire and it's varying fortunes is to be found in the coins, owing to the custom of issuing money from many of the most important provincial centres, as well as at the capital, and of recording on the coin the mint from which it was issued....The coins, therefore, form a valuable adjunct to the plentiful, but often unsatisfactory, historical records of the Mughal period...My aim has been to let the coins illustrate themselves, how, from a small kernel – the principality of Kabul – the tree of Mughal empire grew strong enough for its branches to cast their shadow over the greater part of the Indian peninsula, till cumbrous with too much weight it fell stricken by the storms that swept round it, the spoil of Afghan and Maratha, Sikh and Rohilla, French and English. Yet such was the prestige which lingered round the tottering monarchy that its supplanters preferred, by recording the name of the sovereign of Delhi on their coins to retain the semblance of suzerainty which such an issue of coinage implied.'

R.B. Whitehead ICS in The Mint Towns of the Mughal Emperors of India says that 'Systematic research in that branch of Indian numismatics belonging to issues of the Mughal Emperors of India is a growth of recent date. The first papers appearing in the Asiatic Society Journal between the years of 1880-95 contributed by C.J. Rogers of Amritsar...until then 'No attempt to describe coin types and inscriptions' had been made and 'such Mint Lists are of use both to the historian as showing what places were included in the Mughal Empire at various periods, and to the numismatist as a guide in ascertaining whether a coin of a particular unit is known or not known.

Systematic and scientific work in the field of Mughal numismatics date from the appearance of R. Burn ICS tables

(Monograph The Mints of the Mughal Emperors first appeared in ASJ 1904). Under the impetus of his excellent example research has proceeded at a rapid rate. The first Numismatic Supplement appeared in 1904 under the editorship of Mr. H. Nelson Wright, ICS and contained contributions from R. Burn, Dr. G.P. Taylor of Ahmedabad, and from the editor. These Supplements have appeared at intervals since that year and have absorbed much of the recent original work done on the numismatics of northern India…'

This search for coins now ran alongside Henry's ICS career and perhaps the two complimented each other. As he traveled the country in his position of District and Sessions Judge there would have been the opportunity to collect and search out coins. It would have become known that he was on the look out and people would have brought him coins.

Coins were more appreciated. Two hundred years ago every English Country House had a coin collection along with a picture gallery and a library. Greek and Roman coins formed the main part of their collections. Then, when money needed to be raised, because coins needed expertise to be appreciated, they were the first to go. Coins have always attracted a diverse collection of people. Those from every walk of life are found at meetings but the people who specialize in one kind of coin tend not to know anything about any other countries coins.

FIRWOOD, CLEVEDEN

In 1907 Henry published The Sultans of Delhi and Mediaeval Muhammadem States.

The Book was most probably completed at Firwood.

Underneath his name, at the end of the Introduction, it says Cleveden 1907. The Rent Roll lists Miss Stuckey as the tenant of Firwood from 1906. Mary Ann Phillips Stuckey made her will in 1906 though it is thought she died five years later since Probate was filed on 13 February 1911. The lease was in any case taken on by Mrs. Nelson Wright and for the next 20 years Firwood became their British base and as stable a home as any the family would ever know. From then on wherever they lived in India or elsewhere their home address was given as Firwood, Cleveden.

The house lends itself to settled, civilized life. The pink painted, Regency House with well proportioned rooms built in 1830 was Dower House (which is now its name) to Clevedeon Court owned by the Elton family from the 18th century. The two houses were connected by an old wooden footbridge, which crossed Highdale Road, and a path which continued through the grounds.

Firwood had a garden full of plants collected by the Eltons and behind woods that join up with those of Cleveden Court. The House was situated above Highdale Road, on the side of a hill looking across to the Mendip Hills with a distant view of the Bristol Channel. Edmund Elton started his famous pottery in the garden at Firwood before moving his kiln to Clevedon Court when he inherited the title in 1883 (the house is now owned by the National Trust). Edmund was a friend of the family and acted as guardian to the two youngest Nelson Wright boys when they started school at Clifton College.

The Parents had returned to India and were staying at the hill station of Mussourie by the time their third child Innes was born on 31st July 1904. His godfather was Henry's coin collecting friend R.B. Whitehead known as Bertie. However they were back at Firwood when a fourth child and third son Trevor was born on 12th June 1906. His religious protection was given another friend, the Governor of the United Provinces, Sir John Stanley. Unlike Harcourt the two younger boys were sent to Clifton College, perhaps a reflection of the Bristol base. Perhaps because the ICS contributed to the fees which were cheaper than Eton. It was also a school with strong connections to the Stuckey family and Anglo India.

Henry's grandson Anthony Condon said of children in India 'They were all sent home to school in England. Everybody sent their children back to school. There wasn't anywhere to educate them in India, that was really the snag. There weren't any schools, none at all.'

NUMISMATIC SOCIETY

In 1908 Henry compiled another impressive volume on coins The Mughals of India. It was published in Oxford Meanwhile he wrote numerous articles on coins for the Asiatic Society Journal and its supplements. And then in May 1909 he received another promotion to the Legislative Department of the Government of India. From 1910 to 1912 he was Legal Remembrancer to the government of the United Provinces. Also in 1910 he was appointed the editor of what had now become a regular supplement to the Asiatic Society's journal from 1910 to 1924. The first issue being devoted to Rare Mughal Coins.

The Numismatic Society of India was formed on 28 December 1910 in Henry's house in Allahabad. A group of coin collectors decided to formalize their activities and called a Conference at the Residence of the District Magistrate, Henry Nelson Wright and 'resolved to constitute a Numismatic Society of India.' Other members included his life long friend, R.W. Whitehead and H.R. Nevill and Mr. R. Burn. In the Numismatic Supplement No XLI (1928) of the Journal of the Asiatic Society of Bengal it says that, in 1910 Allahabad founded by Sir John Stanley – President, R.B. Whitehead, H.N. Wright, the Numismatic Society of India.

The Society is still in existence today. Dr. Lal Gupta said 'This is now one of the prominent Numismatic Societies and is permanently located in the campus of the Benares Hindu University (Varanesi, U.P.) It holds annual meetings and some prominent numismatist is elected President. Mr. Wright himself was the President on three occasions – Lucknow (19th January 1915); Benares (28 December 1920) and Agra (29th

December 1924).' His Presidential Adrresses were published in a volume: Sixty years of the Numismatic Society of India – published by the Society in 1973.

On the 31 March 1912 a revised list of the Mint Towns, edited by Henry Nelson Wright, appeared in Allahabad. The introduction starts by saying 'The number of the novelties in the Mughal coinage that have come to light since the Numismatic Supplements were started in 1904 is so considerable that it seemed to me that an index of the rarer Mughal coins noticed in the Supplement.

Did the family also return on leave to England that year? There were three kinds of leave. Privilege leave which was the annual one months holiday. Special leave for exceptional reasons. Medical leave – for obvious reasons - and Furlough - long vacations spread over a man's service. The first taken eight years after arrival. They could also take leave on half pay of up to two years. ICS officers generally retired after 25 years service - the maximum being 35 of which six years could be spent on furlough - with a pension.

A reason for taking leave at this time could have been because, in the autumn, his eldest son, Aislerby Harcourt started at Eton. He had attended prep school at Heddon Court, Cockfosters under Mr. H.J. Stallard, and like his father and grandfather, entered Eton on a King's Scholarship. The third generation of the family to do so. A handsome, slightly spoilt looking boy he appears not as brilliant a scholar as his father. A wilder, more chaotic character, good at sports but not chosen for the Wall Game though said to be a scratch golfer and tennis player.

Henry and Edith returned to Allahabad. He is now listed in the Court of Judicial Commissioner, Oudh, Lucknow as moving up from Third Grade to Second Grade.Judge.

The wedding of Isola and William Hunt Condon

Isola and William with their children Michael, Pam, and Anthony.

Did they take Isola with them? She had now left school and the next stage for a girl of her up bringing and background was marriage. She duly met William Hunt Condon, A Royal Artillery Officer and amateur water colourist. What did her parents think of him?

He was the youngest of nine children born to James Hunt Condon, who came from Limerick in Ireland and was then the Brigade Surgeon based in Cawnpur, and Emma Louise the feisty daughter of the well know writer William Knighton. William Hunt Condon was born in 1886 and after an education at Clifton College and Woolwich was commissioned into the Royal Artillery, Officially, at 28, he was too young for marriage – the preferred age was 30 - and the it affected his career. He transferred to the Indian Army for their better pay and joined the 5th/13th Frontier Force Rifles. The couple married in November 1914. The 1st World War had begun and Isola's husband was posted to the Middle East. Isola returned to Firwood where she spent the war sharing the house with her step sister-in-law, Maudie Rennie .and growing family. Michael born 1916, Pamela 1918 and Anthony 1921.

On 29 January 1915 it is recorded that the Annual Meeting of the Numismatic Society was held, under the President Henry Nelson Wright, in Lucknow. There is an important collection of coins in the Lucknow Museum established by Henry and R.B. Whitehead. The Murray Guide says 'The numismatic section, which is almost unique for the period of Greek rule in Bactria and the Punjab, and contains also Muslim and Indian coins of great interest'. The director of the museum was Lockwood Kipling, father of the author Rudyard Kipling, and the museum contained 'a comprehensive collection of musical instruments made by the late Lockwood Kipling, which show great beauty of design.'.

Then in February 1917 the Henry Nelson Wright Medal was instituted for 'outstanding research on numismatics to be given annually'. It is still given annually as far as I am aware. According to Dr. Lal Gupta the award marked his most important discovery 'the gold coin of the Mughal emperor Jehangir, depicting the portraits of his father Akbar. This coin is now in the British Museum and, so far, it is the only known specimen. The numismatic Society of India has instituted a medal showing this coin, in the name of Mr. Wright. The medal was originally engraved by an English engraver in London. He retained the die and supplied medals to the Society when needed. During World War ll, the Society lost the track of the engraver. So, the medal was re-engraved by an Indian artist; the new medal is now awarded and known as 'Nelson Wright Medal'

At some point this year Henry and Edith returned to Britain. The last photographs of the family was taken at Firwood and shows Harcourt in army uniform and the two younger boys, Innes and Trevor in their Clifton school uniform. Edith is wearing a lavish dress and Henry a wing collar and a solemn, paternal look. Harcourt had entered Sandhurst straight from Eton and then he joined The Somerset Light Infantry and was posted to Ireland.

Was the reason for their return to Britain because Henry had been offered a job at the India Office in London; or because Edith was suffering from cancer and he asked for a transfer?

On 13 December 1917 Edith died of cancer, probably at Firwood. The address on her Will is given as Firwood How long did she suffer? How long in advance did they know she was dying? What kind of cancer? Was Isola there? Was Harcourt? All these questions could have been asked and answered but one never thought to inquire and now it is too late. Edith's name was never mentioned. Perhaps this is significant. Perhaps my grandmother Isola was too devastated by her mother's death and subsequent events to talk to a grandchild who might not understand.

Edith's Will leaves all to her 'beloved husband' apart from bequests to the children and she changed her mind twice - writing two codicils. And twice she states that precautions should be taken so that she is not buried alive.

Harcourt left for the France and the Front on August 15th, 1918. In September Henry was in the Lake District staying at the Kendal Hotel when he received a telegram forwarded on from Firwood. It was from the War Office and said 'I deeply regret 2nd Lt. A.H. Wright 1st Somerset Light Infantry killed in action September 2nd, 1918. The army council expresses sympathy. Signed Secretary War Office.' A second telegram from the King and Queen at Buckingham Palace followed and then a letter from his commanding officer explaining the situation in the best possible light. After this came the letters Harcourt had written from the Front, telling of his dreadful journey and the lack of food and sleep.

The truth was that Harcourt had been blown to bits by a stray shell that hit the men in the assembling yard. There was no glorious or heroic battle to mitigate his death. It was just a senseless waste. There was not even a grave to visit. He became a name in a list on Panel 4 at the Vis-en-Artois Memorial in the British Cemetary on the road between Arras and Cambrai. Henry himself paid for a brass memorial plaque, on a wall at the entrance to the Eton Chapel.

The blow to Henry must have been terrible. And following so soon after Edith's death. One can only think that he was in a state of shock from the grief and loneliness. How else to explain his immediate behaviour which seems completely out of character. He became involved with his landlady's daughter.

RETURN TO INDIA AND REMARRIAGE

While Henry was working at the India Office in London he lodged with Madge Pool and her mother, Mrs. Barnes. Madge was thirty years his junior, the widow of a warrant officer who before the war had been stationed in India and had died – perhaps killed in the war. Anthony Condon says: 'Edith died of cancer in about 1916, but I don't think he was too upset about it. He married again quite quickly. The Judge came home to England on a posting to the India Office. He lived in lodgings and the story is that he married his landlady's daughter, Madge.'

Was this a version of events perpetrated by Madge who perhaps saw a chance of bettering herself with the Judge. Whatever, they married on 25 September 1919.

Madge also took hold of jewelry and possessions that, if Edith's Will were interpreted correctly, should have gone to her daughter Isola. She was shocked both by her father's marriage to a woman of her own age and one who she regarded as a social inferior, and by the deception over the jewels. She retained a life long hatred for Madge but, as Tony said 'think what it would be like if your father married someone younger than you and then gave her all your mother's things. Her clothes and jewelry. And if you regarded her also as socially inferior. She was the landlady's daughter.' Such things mattered in those days.

Isola had returned to India for, on 21st May 1918, her daughter Pamela was born in Jubblepore. Perhaps that was the reason she did not fight harder for her rights. It was difficult at long distance and the War must have further slowed down communications.

Her brothers Innes and Trevor also suffered from the second marriage and losing the support of their mother. Madge resented any money being spent on the children. After Clifton Innes went up to Oxford studied Divinity at Keble College, then became a clergyman but disliked the role and started to teach. He ended up at the prep school Durlston Court as master for French and Divinity. In the holidays he took parties of boys to Switzerland and visited his aunt Polly living in Montreux. Trevor was sent to train as an accountant and when he disliked the trade and asked to transfer to Law was told there was no money for further education and through contacts joined Dunlop. He did marry and had a son Ian. There was also a daughter who died in infancy.

Henry and Madge returned to India soon afterwards where the ICS also made plain their disapproval of the marriage. 'The ICS was not Madge's world and she didn't know anything about it and she didn't fit it.' Ian Nelson Wright says 'I do remember that he had problems when he went back because Madge had been the wife of a warrant officer. She had been married before in India. The wife of a warrant officer was not acceptable to the hierarchy in that society, so that affected things, I believe.' The Indian Civil Service were not forgiving of any breach of their standards. It was difficult to get sacked but they could make their disapproval known by other means.

Did Harcourt Butler come to his rescue – his old friend and brother-in-law. He was now Governor of the United Provinces and previously Governor of Burma. It says in the official record that on 15 February 1920: Lieut. Gov. Sir Spencer Harcourt Butler KCSI CIE assumed charge of the office of the Court of Judicial Commissioner, Oudh, Lucknow . Henry was appointed Judge lst Grade at the High Court in Bareilly. An acceptable post though Bareilly was not one of the major centres of jurisdiction.

Bareilly was a city to the north of Delhi with a population in 1933 of one hundred and forty four thousand. It had been Capital of the country of Rohilkhand and their headquarters. 'The Rohillas were no less turbulent than other fighting elements in India and took a prominent share in the dismemberment of the Mughal Empire'. Bareilly passed to the British by cession in 1801. They had their share of troubles in the Mutiny but in May 1858 Sir Colin Campbell came to the rescue. In 1871 the city was again disturbed by a series of religious riots. The city contains some fine bazaars and mosques, one dating to Shah Jahan, and was famous for its rows of Bamboos. 'A battery of artillery and an Indian infantry regiment are now quartered in the Cantonment (1933) and it is the headquarters of the 8th infantry Brigade.'

A photograph exists of Henry and Madge, surrounded by members of the court, posed outside the court house in Bareilly. Sitting on Madge's knee is a small girl. Their daughter Joan Alison was born on 12th March 1924 in Bareilly.

From this time on Henry looks old and miserable in his photographs. Gone is the confident, slightly swaggering, good looking man sitting in the centre of the family. Replaced by a stooping figure, standing on the outskirts of the group with a tired, withdrawn expression on his aging face. And the photographs are not large format, studio produced pictures but snap shots taken with a basic camera.

He appears to have buried himself in his coins and the Numismatic Society. There was a meeting in Benares overseen by the President Henry Nelson Wright on 28 December 1920 and another in Agra on the 29 December 1924. He begins compiling books that become standard works on their subjects. Two volumes of a three volume set on the Catalogues of coins in the Indian Museum Calcutta: 'In the year 1906 1st Vol of new catalogue of coins in the India Museum, Calcutta by Mr. Vincent A Smith ICS (retired), on the pre-Muhammedan series, and this has been followed by the second and third volumes dealing respectively with the issues of the Pathan Sultan of Delhi and their contemporaries, and with those of the Mughal Emperors of India. Both have been written by Mr. H. Nelson Wright ICS.'

In an address to the Series of Pathan Coins Mr. Geo. P. Taylor says 'The majority of coins of the Suri Sultans, a period which, apart from the important change in the character of the currency on Sher Shah's accession, and the beauty and variety of the coins themselves, is of peculiar interest to the numismatist by reason of the expansion of the mint system, through which the collector is enabled both to direct the interest of the antiquary towards deserted and forgotten cities or erstwhile importance, and also to help the historian in fixing the limits and extent of these sovereigns' dominions by confirming and supplementing the scanty materials on which he has to rely.'

The sorting of the coins in the Calcutta Museum had been a herculean task. First Mr. Rogers laboured to arrange 7.000 coins, higgledy-piggledy' The job took two years, then Mr. H. Nelson Wright took over 'with infinite patience and accuracy marshaled numerous details, but he has grouped and correlated them with singular skill. One scarcely knows which more to admire, the ample stock of minute information or its lucid presentation....He has indeed, made a distinct forward movement...Mr. Wright, by boldly adventuring to follow a new principle of classification, has immensely enhance the usefulness of his book as a practical working catalogue. First the coins are grouped under the different Emperors; next the coins of each Emperor are separated according to their metal, gold or silver or copper; and lastly under each Emperor the coins of each metal are classified according to their mints, the several members of these mint-sub-groups being arranged chronologically. Here, then, we have a distinctly scientific presentment of the coins issued in different years from each mint during each reign.' Ahmadabad: 1st August 1908.

For the Provincial Museum at Lucknow Henry produced a Catalogue of Coins of the Sultans of Delhi to which he writes a foreword. It was published in Allahabad in 1925 and the coins Henry collected are still to be seen in the museum. Henry writes: Lucknow Museum contains 1,045 coins of a period known as Sultan of Delhi compared with 899 in the Indian Museum in 1907 Catalogue and 640 in the British Museum 1884 Cat. It takes time to produce a catalogue: 'A provincial cabinet labours under many disadvantages. It is seldom anybody's child. It has to rely almost exclusively on acquisitions from casual finds, brought within its reach by the provisions of Treasure Trove. It is generally a very uneven collection and its strength likely to lie rather in completeness of its series of the commoner coins of the locality than in possession of many specimens of outstanding rarity. For the acquisition of later systematic search and liberal expenditure are a sine qua non.

But these two essentials are seldom forth coming in a public institution. 'The Lucknow Museum was more fortunate than some sister museums. It has a strong committee of experts, enthusiastic numismatists and possesses a curator who thanks to his own industry has acquired a numismatic instinct. It only remains for him to afford extended facilities for personal travel and research.

Lucknow Museum is strong on coins of Khyaljis and the three principal Sultans of Tughlong. For after all where is a numismatic study of the coinage of the Sultans of Delhi more entitled to look for his materials than to the Museum of the Province in which that coinage was current.'

Several years later, in 1936 the Coinage & Metrology of the Sultans of Delhi was published by the Government of India Manager of Publications, New Delhi 1936. 'This latter work is an important one and Mr. Wright is well known for it', according to Venetia Porter at the British Museum who said in 1994 that it was still used by the Coin Department as their standard reference book.

Henry continued to write papers published in the Numismatic Supplements. 'You may refer to their list Bibliography of Indian Numismatics (Muhammaden Series) by C.R. Singhal, published by the Society. 'From it you may have the exact references of their publication. I think all the above publications are available in the Coin Department of the British Museum.'

After five years at the High Court in Bareilly Henry retired. He had done thirty five years service with the I.C.S. longer than most for whom 25 years was the norm. He would have received the ICS pension which, in 1820 was set at £1000 a year. Generous in those days but as the years progressed and the cost of living rose, the pensions remained the same. So in 1925 it was not a great sum and if he had never saved, money could have been in short supply. 'Civilians were notoriously bad at saving money, spending much on school fees and entertaining and often neglecting to make arrangements for their family when they died. Few Civilians had private means, few would have joined the ICS if they had.' According to Ian Nelson Wright, Henry was offered a title, as was customary with retiring ICS officers, but turned it down saying 'I have only done my duty.'

RETIREMENT

Henry, Madge and Alison returned to England and first rented a house in north London. 42 Ravenscourt Road, Golder's Green. (Or was this the house belonging to Madge's mother Mrs. Barnes where Henry originally lodged?) Henry then bought a large timber framed, mock Tudor house with a tennis court in the garden at Upper Warlingham. The Larches was chosen for its proximity to London and the British Museum where he helped to catalogue their coin collections.

Henry and Madge often travelled on the Continent. Trevor wrote to them every week and his letters survive, addressed to places all over Europe, especially Italy, Whatever the outside-opinion of Madge she was obviously kind and hospitable to Henry's grand children. Pam (daughter of Isola) remembers spending school holidays with them and her being kind. Anthony regarded their home as the only one he had in Britain. He often stayed with them during his school holidays and remembers traveling by tube down from Golder's

Green to the British Museum. 'The Judge was immensely kind to me and used to take me to sights like the Tower all over London He had fallen out with his children over his wife… She was thirty years younger than him. A very bossy lady. She used to boss him about and treat him like a child. They had one child, a daughter Alison. We were brought up with Alison. She was only two or three years older than me. I used to spend part of each holidays with them at their house, The Larches at Upper Warlingham in Surrey where they moved.

Innes and Trevor Nelson Wright

Michael, his eldest grandson, also recalls him as 'A highly distinguished man who didn't cast a vote in the household. A small, insignificant man.' Michael rejects my statement that he became a High Court Judge. 'He didn't have the personality to be a high court judge'. Michael also never remembers him mentioning anything about coins but that may have been because he 'probably thought coins too esoteric a subject for anybody of Michael's age. He was quiet and scholarly without much character. But then he was browbeaten by his wife.'

Anthony repeats that 'The Judge was a very withdrawn man. He had two passions, gardening – he grew rock plants – and collecting coins. He also collected butterflies. He spent all his time doing that or traveling up to London to the British Museum to catalogue coins. The Larches was bought because it was accessible to London and the British Museum. He had what amounted to the best collection of antique Indian gold coins outside the British Museum. He used to go up to the British Museum regularly and he helped catalogue their collections.

Tony said 'I have never tried to see them but they must be still there. They must have been worth a fortune. Perhaps they were given to the British Museum.' In fact they were given to the British Museum and the Coin Museum in Delhi (which he founded together with Bertie Whitehead and others) on the condition the coins were kept together as a collection and not broken up.

The Judge was not a handy man and lacked any practical abilities. 'He could hardly change a light bulb let alone a fuse or a plug.' He never learned to drive a car.

Whereas in India there were servants to perform these tasks, in England they didn't have any living in servants, but of course they did have a cook. They weren't very well off. He hadn't made any money in India. Or if he did I don't know what he did with it. He had this very valuable coin collection and he might have spent all his money on coins. He must have inherited a certain amount from his parents, but I really don't know much about his background. He never struck me as being a man of very strong character, but he had been domineered by his second wife.'

June Eggleston (a grand niece) remembers him as 'Balding and he wore small gold rimmed glasses. A retiring person who was really a bit self effacing. He was a considerable Arabic Scholar,' who also spoke Hindi and Urdu.

His activities in the coin world continued and he became a Fellow of the Royal Numismatic Society in London. In 1932 he was awarded the Numismatic Society's Medal and his services to Indian Numismatics were commemorated by a special gold medal. In 1936 he gave an address to the London Society and In India the Coinage & Metrology of the Sultans of Delhi was published by the Government of India Publications in New Delhi.

Harcourt Butler died from heart disease and gout in The Hospital for Tropical Diseases, St. Pancras on 2nd March 1938. He had retired from India to a small flat in the Temple where he lived alone but with a large circle of friends. The list in the Times of people attending his funeral includes Lady Butler and Henry Nelson Wright but his widow is missing from the Memorial Service. Florence was remembered in his Will. The chief beneficiary was his son Victor but after him -'to my wife

Amy Florence Katherine Lady Butler the sum of two hundred and fifty pounds'..

Anthony Condon says, 'My mother and Lady Butler did not get on and so we never saw that side of the family. But was the estrangement begun by Henry? Did he disapprove of Florence's treatment of her husband and his friend Harcourt? Or perhaps she disapproved of his marriage? There is no mention of her in his later life and no bequest in his will.

Gardening continued to be an engrossing occupation. It is noticeable that he chose to specialize in rock plants. Like coins, they are small plants requiring minute attention. He seems to have retired from the world and become to outward appearances an insignificant man bullied by his younger wife. The age difference began to tell and, remaining a sociable person herself and nearer to her step children and grand children in age, Madge often commandeered one to escort her to events. Trevor remembers several such occasions and Michael.

In spite of the fact that Henry spent his time going up to the British Museum, his grand children hardly knew of his interest in coins let alone the authority with which he as held in that world. Was this another method that Madge used to humiliate and control her elderly husband. And perhaps this was a reason that Edith was never mentioned. As a way of exerting her control, discussion of her predecessor was forbidden.

Henry became ill with cancer. In 1941 Tony went to visit him in hospital before sailing for India to join the war effort. 'I was in the army at the time, awaiting embarkation orders for India and I remember going to see him in hospital at

Caterham which was near Upper Warningham' It was the last time he saw the Judge. He died on 13 May 1941 aged 71.

He made a Will on 6 March 1940. The executors were his widow and her former brother in law Frederick Eldred Pool, Lieutenant Colonel R.E. M.B.E. HM Army. Henry did not leave a fortune - the net value of the personal estate amounted to £121.1.7 The house was to be sold and the proceeds divided between Madge and Alison. There were bequests to his children and sister Polly but none to Florrie. And what remained of Edith's estate was to go to his children. The Will is matter of fact and straight forward. There are no expressions of emotion.

The Numismatic Society of India paid him a tribute. Rai Bahadur Prayag Dayal made an address reprinted in the Journal of the NSI Vol 111, 1941 (p 137-38) in which he said 'Mr. Nelson Wright, I.C.S. (retd.), whose death was reported with some delay owing to the war conditions by the Times of India, dated 17th October 1941, passed away on 13th May 1941, at his house in Surrey at the ripe old age of 71…one of the foundation members of the NSI and the first editor of its Numismatic Supplement. His association with the Society since its inception in 1910 up to his retirement from India in 1924 contributed in a substantial manner to its prosperity and expansion, particularly in the early stages. He will long be remembered for his sound researches in Muslim numismatics as embodied in Vols. 11 & 111 of the coin catalogue of the India Museum and in his latest standard work on the Coinage and Metrology of the Sultans of Delhi which is a corpus on the subject. His connection with our Society is perpetuated in the form of the Nelson Wright Medal founded by him to be awarded annually for a contribution on Indian Numismatics of outstanding merit. "I am specially reminded on his last words while leaving India in relation to the Society, when he exhorted us not to let it die of inaction. The message has served as an inspiration to me throughout, and I am glad to say that the Society has lived up to his words and has witnessed an all round steady progress."

AFTERMATH

In April 1995 his grand daughter Pam (Isola's daughter who married Maj. Gen. R.E. Urquhart who commanded the 1st Airborne Divison at the Battle of Arnhem in 1944) and her daughter Judith (myself) visited the British Museum, having requested to see the coin collection. One reason was that I was doing research into the family's Indian connections before traveling from Calcutta to Peshawar in their footsteps.

We were met by Venetia Porter from the Department of Coins. When asked, among other questions, from where Henry Nelson Wright got the coins: she answered that they would have come from dealers. It would have been known that he was interested and people would bring him coins. In the field of Islamic or Mughal – to distinguish them from Hindi – he is really highly regarded. He was a great pioneer in the field. His work is incredibly useful and still stands today. We consult his books all the time. He really knew his stuff. Some of the coins would have been incredibly difficult to read especially if they had never been read before. It is easy once someone has done the initial deciphering, spade work to continue. It is making a start that is impossible. Some had very difficult inscriptions. There was a group of them – Whitehead and Burn who he would have consulted. They all worked together and produced different volumes. Not much work had been done on establishing the Islamic coins.

He gave, or he may have sold, the coins to the British Museum in batches at different times. The gold coins are obviously the most attractive and would have been the most valuable, especially the zodiacal coins. He also gave silver and copper coins.'

It is notable that one major batch was donated in 1939. Two years before he died. Did he know he was suffering from cancer that no one would appreciate his previous coins? That they would have been sold. Because that was all that was remembered by his family of this scholarly man: that he was interested in coins and used to visit the British Museum. Venetia Porter was plainly shocked by how little we knew. And I began to equally feel ashamed. Though she did admit that the Museum knew little of him as a person

In the Museum the coins were kept stacked in high tunnels of polished mahogany cases interspersed with shelves of books. Slim drawers with ivory button handles that pull out to reveal coins laid in separate circles, each slot categorized and each resting on a little round label with the name of the donor and the date when donated. H. Nelson Wright in black capital letters could be detected under coin after coin.

Beautiful, bright gold circles inscribed with Islamic calligraphy or the sign of the zodiac of perfect precision. Some of the coins were square and some more precious had the Emperor Jehangir's head in profile. They depicted a change of reign. And on the top shelf were his books. 'I am ashamed at how worn they are' said Venetia Porter. The covers were going on some 'but that is because they are used so often'. One or two had been given by his widow and had her name inscribed in the front.

I followed Venetia Porter's advice and wrote to Dr. Lal Gupta at the Indian Numismatic Society and visited the library of the Asiatic Society. There they appeared to have all Nelson Wright's books and articles on coins. Sitting in the gloom of an afternoon I read the introductions. Even though they were exclusively on the subject of coins I began to get a picture of the man. It was the way he stated his opinions. Very correct, decisive and dictatorial. You felt the effect of a highly intelligent, legal mind. One used to weighing up facts and producing verdicts. But also precise, painstaking, seeing both sides of the coin – literally – making deductions, drawing conclusions. A deeply scholarly mind, which could study the flowing lines of Arabic inscriptions and understand their waves. He must have seen in the calligraphy, meanings and other worlds.

I had heard he was a quiet, introverted man and thought perhaps his solace was found deep in the world of the coins; in the one their inscriptions and their mint towns conjured up. Through them he could imagine the lavish romance of the courts of the Mughal Kings. The machinations of courtiers and politicians. The movement of armies. Empires rising and falling, towns being established, merchants beginning to travel, transactions between financiers and money lenders and all by the Will of Allah. Because the obverse of every coin contained a plea for his good will.

His real world sounded dull and disappointing. His wife was bossy and his children were uninterested. The coins gave him a place for retreat. He could retire into the world they recreated. Into the Coin Department at the British Museum, hide in the stacks, with its rows of little drawers filled with round coins, where what mattered was minute differences of scholarly interpretation. And at the end of a day, spent out of this world and in one with more of a feast to feed the imagination, he returned home and lost himself in the world of his garden with its plants and butterflies.